DIV][DED

THE HUMAN SIDE OF US

Dedicated to My heart
My Mother
Your love is the only thing that
cannot be divided

INTRODUCTION

*h*ave you ever felt like you don't really know who you are? Or have you ever gone out with your friends and had a good time, then came home and asked yourself: "Who was that person? Was that me, or who others *want* me to be?"People often throw around terms like "midlife crisis," "identity crisis," or something along the lines of "I feel lost." But what does that really mean?

According to the dictionary, a **midlife crisis** is defined as a period of psychological stress occurring in middle age, thought to be triggered by a physical, occupational, or domestic event, as menopause, diminution of physical prowess, job loss, or departure of children from the home.

An **identity crisis** is defined as a period of uncertainty and confusion in which a person's sense of identity becomes insecure, typically due to a change in their expected aims or role in society.

According to *my* definition, it all comes down to being confused about … well, everything! It's about feeling lost.

Rather than view what I am going through in a negative light, I have decided to describe what is happening to me as a **"Midlife Bang!"**

So here I am, presumably having a midlife ~~crisis~~ bang in my early thirties, although most who know me would most likely disagree and say things like "You're in a *constant* midlife ~~crisis~~ bang!" and make comments like "You women never know what you want." But does everyone out there really know what they want? Or do we just kind of pretend we do and go with the flow? Or maybe what we want changes over time?

I have watched many of my friends reach the age 30 and, well, "lose it" for a year or so: some quit their jobs and travel, others cut their hair super short, some have babies, and others go live in the forest.

But why? What happens to us when we hit the age 30?

I initially tried to research the topic, but after a few hours, I realized that would be a whole book in itself. So rather than trying to understand *why* I seem to have hit a wall at this point in my life, I have decided to take a more modern and Oprah-inspired approach and to think of it as an opportunity to find my true calling!

Why The Divided?

I'd like to start by telling you a little about what this whole "divided" thing is about and, well, why I am sharing it with you.

I drew a little illustration for you to highlight some of the conflict that makes me feel divided.

I recommend that you also draw an illustration of all the things that make you who you are!

My illustration:

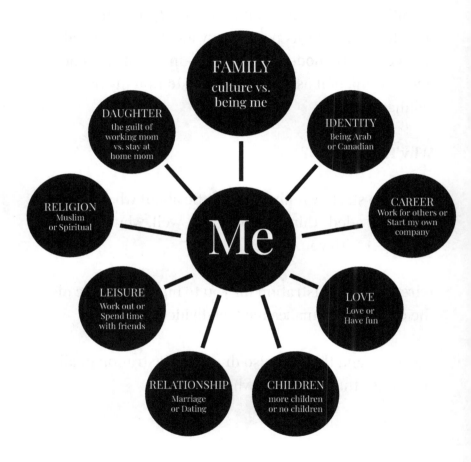

Your illustration:

After drawing this illustration, I made a list of all the things I consider to be the "core" of who I am, so I suggest you do the same, and in the process of trying to figure out who you are or what you want, you could maybe focus on these things to keep you grounded.

Me and my core

I am an Arab Muslim Canadian and have lived the majority of my life in my now forever home, Canada. That being said, I have a strong relationship to my culture and my people, this connection that has never faded and will likely never fade. So I have taken on this Canadian identity while at my core maintaining a Middle Eastern heart.

Over the years and until now, I have been divided between these two identities, as I do not fit in with Canadians, nor do I really fit in with Arabs. I am both, and somehow neither. It's like a new culture has formed, one that encompasses a mixed background and mixed understandings of life and being. The people I do seem to get along with are ones who like me have experienced this divide in their life, which can happen with people from all backgrounds: Russian Canadian, Bosnian Canadian, Persian Canadian, Indian Canadian, etc. We all somehow have this understanding by just looking at one another, an understanding of a divide that's within us between who we are with others and who we are at heart. While some have found a balance that works for them, I am still struggling to do so.

People are always telling me that I am stubborn and that I question things too much. That I should stop questioning and start accepting. But how can I stop questioning? The moment I stop questioning is the moment I stop learning, and I will NEVER stop learning. If I don't learn I don't evolve, and if don't evolve then I won't survive.

I question everything. All the time.

Have you ever performed a cultural ritual or taken part in a cultural tradition, but stopped yourself and said: "This makes no sense whatsoever?"

Or has an uncle ever said something that was so ignorant, but you could not correct him because he is the eldest, and no one must ever speak back to him?

These things happen—**all the time**—and while society imposes all these identities on us that we try to keep up with, we come home to a different set of expectations.

As a woman with a strong cultural background, I have to try to respect that aspect of my life while also trying to succeed as one of the only female executives in my company. I have to manage the many faces I must wear to ensure I maintain my (self-) respect, my power and my opinions.

Life has placed expectations on all of us. Who we should be? How we should be? What we need to be? From the moment you are born, your parents start telling you what you should and should not do, whom you should and should not be, how you should speak and when not to speak. Then all of sudden, you are let out into the world and faced with a new set of societal rules that are telling you who and how and what you should be. Finally, you wake up one day, look in the mirror and ask yourself: "Who do *I* want to be?"

This is what I call my **Midlife Bang**!

The bang is a blessing if you decided to give into it, because this is where you begin to slowly cast off the chains that have shackled you throughout your life, the little (and not so little) voices that say "don't do this" and "don't do that," and "be like this" and "don't be like that." This is where you start breaking those chains one link at a time and making your own rules, deciding who YOU want to be, who you were meant to be and who God put you on this earth to be. Our life had supposedly began with a bang, and so in this case, your Midlife Bang can just be the beginning of a new life.

Although I could keep going about the struggles and the contradictions that we carry with us throughout our life, I wanted to share some of my writing that helped me cope with the pressures of trying to be a certain way. I always challenged what I was told and tried to find my own way, but have struggled with feeling divided, with trying to make decisions while trying to understand my true self, who I am and what is right for me, not what others see as right.

This journey has been painful, and the struggle won't ever fully be over, but I take the struggle and burn it as fuel to keep growing, to keep learning and to keep inspiring others to be who they truly are, to find their authentic self and their own voice in life.

I have created a questionnaire to help you answer some questions for yourself, and maybe through these questions you can start planning the next few chapters of your life, then the next, and to slowly keep moving forward.

1. Who am I? (describe biologically who you are,

physically who you are, and emotionally who you are)

2. What are the three things I value most about myself?

3. What are the three things I value most in life?

4. What are three things about myself that I would like to improve?

5. Who do I look up too?

6. Where do I see myself in 5 years? (physically, emotionally, career, relationships, and spiritually)

7. What do I feel divided about?

8. List 3 things you can start doing to understand yourself more?

9. What do you do for self love? And if you don't, why?

I don't have it all figured out, but I have at least seen the root of what divides me, and in seeing it I try to understand it, and by understanding it, I accept it, and through accepting it I can let it go.

In order for us to try to understand our present self, we must look back at our past self, and through the understanding of the present and past we can better plan out the future. In trying to understand myself better, I had to look back at my past. Fortunately, I loved writing, and so I wrote to heal, I wrote to express, and I wrote to relate.

These writings were compiled over the years from childhood onward. I stopped writing poetry when I got married, had my daughter and got caught up in life. However, I never gave writing up completely and started writing letters to my daughter while pregnant, which I still do to this day. Writing has been an escape for me. No matter how busy life gets, I try to find the time to pass on knowledge to my daughter regarding experiences that I face and I do my best to pass on any knowledge I can to those around me.

Through this Midlife Bang, one of the exercises I did was to revisit my past so I could understand myself better and come to terms with it in order to move forward. When I began compiling this book and every time I open it, I remember all the stories I heard from people struggling with similar experiences and emotions. Many of my friends have asked me to share these writings with them, and each one related to them differently and in their own way.

When reading my writing, please do keep in mind that the majority of them were stories of other people. When hearing their stories I was emotionally touched, and so I wrote to express those emotions.

As part of the process of *me* finding who *I* am, I wanted to share these writings with you in the hope that they might help *you* find *you* by facing your own struggles and emotions by facing your own divide. Only in facing them will you conquer them.

This book is divided into two sections; The Heart and The Mind, the two places we face the most divide in.

In section one of the book (The Heart), the poems speak to our emotional side. I urge you to embrace your emotions, allow yourself to feel love, to feel pain, and all of the emotions that come with your life. Feel through them so you are able to let them go.

In section two of the book (The Mind) the poems spoken more through the rational mind.

We as human will always have the divide between the heart and the mind, which one wins is up to you to decide. But remember it is you who is writing the chapters of your story.

I wish you all the best on your journey.

THE HEART

Embrace the journey..

Anger

This next poem is one that is very dear to my heart. After years of abuse in all kinds, I was finally able to get out, and have a chance at a new start. In the midst of healing is anger that is beyond what can be imagined, and I used to calm myself in all ways possible and so I poured it out in the next poem.

If my anger was unleashed mountains would move
For a God made man could not handle its Roar

Its echo would break down his molecules and shatter the
very Ego he used to cause it

He will not bare the truth about his being
The truth that broke the essence in me

But God made a woman strong enough
to bare what no man can
See, it's a woman who carried him, fed him,
and raised him
Only to stand in-front of one someday and say "Listen
woman
Now that you have made me I am above you and a step
ahead of you, I know what's best for you and what you
should do"

Reminds me of a story from the rituals they use where the devil stood in front of his creator and said I am better than him (Adam).
I am made of fire and he of dust

Well the devil came to MAN and said you are better than her so hit her with truth that you cant bare so she knows her place, and if she rejects it then your fist she shall face

He forgot who carried him into this world and through it, lifted his fist and showed her what her Worth is Only to realize that fists and words might break her for a while, but she was made of light and fire, and God's essence in her will help her build an empire

My anger, I ask you to sleep,
for there is no better way to kill a sheep
Let his ego overtake him and watch as Life passes him.
I promise you it will show on his face, and the very
essence that created him will slowly diminish him.

Confused

A friend of mine once came to me lost in his own thoughts. He felt like no one truly understood him and what he was trying to achieve. He confided that he never felt like he really fit in and that he often felt alone. I reassured him that regardless of how different he felt, he should never stop trying to follow his dreams and should always be himself. I wrote this for him to make him feel better, since he was a fan of my writing and told me I should one day become a writer and influence millions. I smiled and said that I hoped that my words could influence one person for now and maybe one day they would influence a million. He went on to become a very different person while remaining true to himself. He is now a doctor who although never fit in, has found his calling and is trying his best to change the world.

Flawless eyes
Deep stares
Hopeless past
Determined days

He looks around wanting change
Change in his hand ambitious in his mind
Tried to act
Hopes to represent
For he does not know that people around just pretend

He thinks they see, but they're blind
He hears them speak, but they have no sound
He tries to see through them, but there is no light
He tries to show them, but they don't understand
He speaks to them, but they don't comprehend

Revolving views sometimes makes him confused
But joe will continue to do what he does
Because of his capabilities no one has a clue

Never Crying Eyes

Although very young, in this next piece I had already experienced one-sided love. I was divided between the beautiful world I am surrounded by and the dark emotional world my experience has left me with.

Butterflies dancing
Air whispering through the tree
The sky blue and the birds are flying free
Mountains are standing tall
And bits of leaves are ready to fall

Boats swaying on deep blue waves
Ocean whistling through empty space
Gold shadows covering the place
Coming from the sun's shinning face

Lying on green carpets that covered the ground
With flowers sleeping and birds of sweet sound
Under huge monsters I lay as their green faces
Blocked out the gold shadows coming towards my face

With nothing on my mind but the
birds' sound and giant waves
Came along his gorgeous smile and sparkling eyes
Laid a frown on my lasting smile
For I cannot forget his torturing words
But loving heart
Tricky eyes but deep stares
His unfaithful promises but unthinkable plans
His undesirable thoughts but irresistible mind
His nothing but everything

Gold shadows turned into silver
Whispers turned into screams
Tall mountains became short
And birds with unheard sound

My face became emotionless and heart became black
For he has erupted the volcano inside
Sucked out all the honey and left an empty hive
With no other to think about
I'm stuck in the sea that filled his eyes
And nothing can bring me out but
A tear from his never crying eyes

Painting

In relationships they say sometimes love blinds you.
I don't think it's love that blinds you, but I believe
that we see in people parts of us, sometimes they are
parts we need to heal, sometimes parts we need to
expand. Now, those are not the forever relationships,
but those are the ones who get you ready for your
true relationship, the one you will call partnership.
How many of you have met someone, only to realize
the picture you have painted of them is so much
more different than who they are? Now look back to
that person, and try to understand if the picture you
painted was of you and not so much of them.

You speak to me of unfulfilled promises
Your words are cold and razor sharp

Trying to get back into the dome of what might be
The point of addiction that made me blind
To your foolishness and lack of pride
I painted a fake picture of who you are

My heart echoes your name
In the darkness of this night
My body remembers the pain
Of that night

I try to forgive you through the tears
But you stole away the last of what I had

You said I was a diamond
A diamond doesn't break but it can get lost
Lost in the two worlds that seem to collide
Of the love I had in its pureness and the wounds that
carve my soul

I never seen beauty in so much pain
Because that same pain holds your name
A name I wanted to carry in the same veins that hold my
blood
And the flesh that could become
I hurt not sure from the love or the pain
But both are beautiful somehow yet in some way

Be Silent

It's one thing to truly understand and feel God, and a whole different thing to try to describe him. I have often felt so full of love and joy that it overflows and it's simply from just loving God and all that he has created. People seemed to not understand this, so through writing I tried my best to explain God in simple terms, although it does not do him justice. For those of you that don't want to call it God, it's that energy that drives our universe and the flow of it. It's PURE love.

His soul, yes his soul
Like an ocean in deepness and mystery
Covers itself with such intimidating waves,
yet such calm nights
His touch is like that of a gentle ocean breeze
His thoughts resemble the calm sea waves
moving along the sand
His emotions are the giant waves
crashing the shore's still rocks

Shhhhhhhhhhhhhhhh
Yes, that's him the silence of the night
Yes, that's him
The sound of air through the trees
Wait, stay still
That's him, the sun's rays through the shade
The sound of early morning birds
The sound of a volcano, an empty one whose eruption
has long passed

Shhhhhhhhhhhhhhhhhhh
That's him
The falling star in the night sky
The sound of rain drops on the ground
The colors of a rainbow

Behold
That's him, the spark in an orphan child's eye
The innocence of a newborn
The kiss of a mother
The arm of a father
Yes, that's him
THE GRACIOUS ALMIGHTY GOD

Prayer

A Prayer can never go wasted, because the God essence in you will answer in so many more ways than one. Here I was praying for God to help me leave a toxic, abusive, and manipulative person. In the freedom of this person leaving your life, comes pain of the person you have loved during the good times.

I kneel before you
As humble as I can be
Grateful for all that you have given me, blessed to be free

I have asked you to rid him of me
I have prayed for this
It is here now but there is pain to endure
No soul can reach its potential nor fulfill its mission
without enduring the hardships of growing

See when your body grows it aches
And so when your soul pains it's growing

*What's more beautiful than your soul growing, your
mind flowing and you'll finally be aligned
With the mighty, the source, the universe, with God*

Brush my Hair

Tired of the world outside and fed up with a society that has turned women into objects and tools, the woman in this next poem is divided between her emotional needs and her material ones. She is using the metaphor of someone brushing her hair as a symbol for someone giving her affection and time to truly enjoy her existence. Ultimately, everyone is divided between love and the material world, and love in its purest form lacks material expectations and can be shown in the simplest of gestures, such as brushing someone's hair.

My birthday was yesterday
You're the best gift I could ask for
I have a gift for you today

Here you go baby
It's a brush, yes a brush
Will you brush my hair?
Tuck me in and make me smile
Even when you're not there
Brush my hair for me baby
Just for five minutes, or forever maybe

With every movement you make
So much hurt away your take
Brush my hair for me baby
Take me in your arms and hug me baby
The world is scary and I've been getting confused lately
This brush is my medication
It holds secrets that I want only you to know
It holds feelings that only you I want to show
Brush my hair baby

More feminine than in this moment, I have never felt
My heart skipped a beat, my body hot wants to melt
See ...
You brushing my hair makes me feel like a woman
Because out on the street I'm a sex object
Men devouring me with their eyes
Raping me with their stares
Trying to fool me with their lies
To persuade me with their money and cars
But they've left me with unwanted scars
Brush my hair baby

As the brush moves along
I get shivers down my spine and feel strong
I've waited for this moment for so long
This brush through my hair
Is the key to ending all of my despair?
This brush through my hair is a lovers' touch
It's making true love
So slow, so deep, so particular
Spreading hair by hair oh so spectacular
No more tangles, nice and smooth
Brush my hair baby

Because I am tired and needing you
Needing to enjoy this magical view
Of you seeing me, my passion and pain,
my love that you never knew
I feel prettier than ever before

See …
When you're not brushing my hair anymore
I become a wave in the endless sea seeking the far shore
This moment will be no more
As you put away the brush, life begins
Hard work, scattered thoughts, focus,
attentions, and pressure

So please
Enjoy the moment, this magical moment
And brush my hair for me baby

Human Touch

This piece is about a woman who has stood strong but is feeling weak and is divided between staying strong and letting her weakness show. You can sense her struggle and feeling of loneliness as she searches for a human touch under which she can let herself be and strip her weakness bare.

Here I stand
Patiently I wait
Eyes looking straight
Arms down by my waist
Heart pumping
Legs trembling
Blood rushing
Hands shaking
Here I stand still waiting
I look strong
Physically I may be
But inside I'm weakening
Have you ever seen a mountain fall?
No!

Look and watch
You'll see one before you just now

Always kept my head high and eyes straight
Always thought I could go against the world
and face fate
Took everything life threw at me like a man
Reminded myself that I'm my only woman

Smiled when I was crying inside
Laughed when I was dying inside
Cried when I was screaming inside
Two worlds are about to collide
The strong me against my weak side

Weakness I am no longer able to hide
Human touch is all I need
The tree is grown and no longer a seed
Even the strongest heart can't survive greed

Look before you
You'll see a woman who's freed
From the chains of life,
She's made her own bitter sweet
Yet still admits to her basic human need
Human touch

Every atom of every inch
Moving along every molecule
Skin tissue against another
Nerves playing together
The feeling of this touch will last forever
Human touch!

Feelings

This one I dedicate to my daughter, and to you when you read it, and remember to just simply love!

If words be feelings
I would be speaking a new language

If stars be far
Then I have reached them

If eyes be precious
Then you can have mine

If hearts be gold
Yours has more shine

If souls be beautiful
Then yours is divine

If minds be incredible
Then yours is desirable

If feelings be real
Then mine are indescribable

Sometimes I Dance

If our bodies were the vessels that hold our souls,
than won't those vessels move to the beat of our life?
Dancing is your soul telling your body to move, so I
urge you to sometimes just stop and dance.

I dance to feel alive
When the world is getting overwhelming
When the noises get loud

I dance to feel the wind
The movements of my arms
The swaying of my hips
Makes me remember that my existence is divine

When was the last time you danced?
Not to the noise of the world but to the silence of your
mind
Not for anyone but just, for you

Stripped Naked

I will let the next piece speak for itself.

I have been stripped naked and it hit me at once
More revealing and freighting than that of the clothes
stripped off your body
Are the layers of illusions that life has covered you with

I stand there feeling naked yet finally existing in the
realm of this universe
Flowing in and out with the divine force of it
Feeling present and light,
still shocked at how covered in layers I was

Your five senses are what makes you, so be careful what
you see, taste, smell and hear. Because it ends up filling
your subconscious with illusions
Layer over another until you become a product of what
you're around

Only love can save you, pure as it comes
When it sees beyond the layers and through
Gives you the strength to strip naked into what was once
the real you

Mirror

I describe this next poem as my soul speaking to me.
Sometimes we look at ourselves and it's like looking
at someone else. They say the eyes are the window to
the soul, so the mirror is the best available means to
help us see through our own eyes and possibly get a
glimpse of our soul.

Look in the mirror
I am your reflection
I am sadness in your eyes
I am endless affection
I am your sorrows and pain

I am your oppressed past running through your vein
I am your tear drop and your smile
I am your heartbeat
I am the YOU that you can't see
I am the YOU that you'll never be
I am your soul
That you are unable to see

Stare

They say the eyes are the window to the soul. How
many times have you randomly ran into someone and
felt a connection just by looking into their eyes?

There is a world in your eyes I want to Discover
Sail across the moment and onto the eternity
that they resemble

I want to dive into them
Go deeper than I could handle
Only to come out to more wonder

I want to feel me in you
Not as a memory but as thunder
So powerful that it makes you shake
like an earthquake where
Your body begins to crumble at the sound of my voice
Your legs weaken to each tone
Your body temperature drops
Your eyes fill up with a spark that screams
- I WANT YOU

Let me dive in to show you me
Let me swim within those mysteries
Let me have you, every bit of you
Even the parts of you that are beyond the physical,
every emotion, every molecule
The good and the bad and the in between,
let me have YOU

Let your eyes intertwine with the beats of my heart until
our soul become one dancing to our union
Let them dance a new form of art that we can call US

Faded Memory

When in the progress of healing from a relationship
that was toxic, you come across many stages of
emotions, this maybe one.

My insides are still residing within you
And so I feel empty on the inside but so full of life
How could this be ?
You took all that is within me
but yet I have never felt so free

Me

Your idea of me does not exist
I am too dynamic to fit within your context

The illusion of the fixed image does not persist
Being human means to co-exist
Not within one system or ideal but from within

I need my inner divide of who and what I am,
where I have been
The different versions over time
that have evolved and grown
The good ones and the ones known as sin
All of them need to learn to co-exist within
Until then I am not your ideal nor mine
I simply exist

Vision

When your vision is aligned with the universe, then potentially the next poem may speak to you.

I am running to you
And because it's you
Every time I fall I get up
When I am down and I look ahead, I see you
When I am tired and lift my head up, I see you
When I can't go anymore and I sit there,
I look ahead and see you

Each time I will get up and run to YOU

You are my home, you are my existence,
you are therefore you are, the all and infinite

I will run forever if it be
Because I know that every time I look up it's you I see

I'll keep running because no vision
is greater than you
Only very few will understand what is YOU

You once said I am therefore I am

I will run and therefore I'll run
Because it is YOU and towards you

I will run

THE MIND
Embrace your Divide...

Fallen for His Charm

The next poem is about a woman who came to this country looking for love and opportunity. Instead, she fell for a charming man who then turned out to be a horrible person. This man abused her and caused her pain. She was divided between her pain and her loneliness, to leave or stay and suffer. However, her ability to overcome her circumstances will radiate courage and strength to many.

Innocent and vulnerable
Thinking the world is tolerable
Trying to live my life honourable
Facing the world not realizing I was so gullible

Came here not knowing a word of English
Not knowing the system not even knowing my place
There were nights I was afraid to sleep because there
were mornings I didn't want to face

Felt like I was out in space
Different galaxies and stars
Big houses and incredible cars

I didn't know where to start
I wanted to be careful and be smart
Got a job waitressing for some cash
Man do my worlds ever clash
Went from being a queen to a nobody
But wait
Maybe a man will make me feel like somebody
Didn't care about looks nor money
Just wanted someone to admire my beauty
Make me feel pretty as he plays with my hair
Makes me feel warm with every touch
Buys me flower to show his care

One is right before my eyes, I can't stop to stare
Ever gorgeous smile and shining eyes
I think I just found the man in those galaxy-filled skies
This one had more depth and shine
I'm going to fight and make him mine
It's been about ten months maybe nine
This man has made me feel so divine

But wait
All of sudden I see rotations
He's angry and filled with frustrations
His words were no longer sweet
His eyes with mine couldn't meet
As he disrespected me with no hesitation
Please not me; there is no way all that was just persuasion

I cried and wept for him
I hurt and pained for him
I stood there and was a woman, a mother, a friend and a father for him
All of sudden nasty names are all I became for him
How could you look me in the eyes and act like you don't care?
Hurt me with words that no other human would bare?
I was lost in my own home I was in constant despair

Not only in a strange land
No, I'm strange in my own home
I'm an immigrant in your arms
I shouldn't have fallen for your charms

You're not a man but a coward
Used my weakness to feel empowered
You used to smell my hair and tell me it's sweet
Now you sniff coke and live on weed
You sold your shoes, what's next the bed sheets
All to find some money, you were a dog on the streets
Broke me once twice and again
Made me feel like everything was made up in my brain
But let me tell you something

This has been your loss and my gain
I came out broke and broken
You're still on the street smoking
I'm living fine and being my best
While you've become a past like the rest
Maybe even dead somewhere
Who knows?

Lesson 1: Don't fall for charm

Lesson 2: Don't stay with a man who's causing you harm

Lesson 3: Never ever underestimate yourself as a woman

An Immigrant
A Victim of War
Maybe a Refugee

One day, while sitting in a social and global issues class, I was listening to the teacher talk about the corrupt political systems and the struggle in third-world countries. It pains me to think of the people that didn't make it. I was lucky to have fled, and as I was escaping with my family, at the age of 6, I witnessed people being caught and shot as we drove away, women and children getting kicked and punched. I remember looking at another girl, maybe 5 or 6 years old, who stared at me as we drove past, her eyes full of terror and fear.

As she stared at me, her father was being kicked on the ground by soldiers. Sitting in the back seat, I was terrified over what I had seen, more so of the fear and despair in her eyes. Fast forward to 26 years later and I still remember this girl, and that terrifying moment and I can't let it go. I don't understand why I made it and she didn't and I promised to dedicate my life to helping those who can't help themselves. In the midst of the pain and confusion about why life is the way it is and why some are suffering for no reason, I wrote this next piece.

Tear drops and pain
Sadness, silence, in vain
Confusion, complications, emotions in constant
circulations
Blood rushing, heart pumping, and twisted ideas in
infinite rotations
Feeling worse than that of starvations of hungry
children in endless incarnation

Thoughts determined but need alterations
All things beautiful even in meaningless creations

Colours and shapes bringing about hesitations
Especially when beings are able to do better imitations
Got their scientists to think beyond limitations
Creating imaginary things, wonders and different
fascinations
Timeless, priceless manifestations
Bird-like creations taking you to all kinds of
destinations
Big buildings, nice cars, English speaking, rich
foundation
This is it the best place for my long dream of migration

I'm in a place of modernization
Tolerance, acceptance, and ethnic affiliation
Time for adaptations, a true refugee determination
Obtain my civil liberties and abuse the system's
integration
The key term of the United Nation's persuasion
Government officials giving fractious, controversial,
idealized, demonized dysfunctional justifications
To second-class citizens who were promised integration

True north strong and free
Wants us all integrative and determined to be
Or at least that's what the IRB wants the world to see
But what no one knows is how hard it is for me
To come from a land across the sea
Where Islam and haram was the way to be
But now faced with a new me
Abortion, contraception, and corruption
Domestic violence, divorce, child custody, depressed
wages, poverty and war against my nations

The media becoming an illness, a disease, wicked and
chronic,
creating false messages that create chaos and moral
panic
Per swaying people that all Muslims are terrorists is
overly problematic
Because it's unrealistic and untrue
I'm a Muslim and I live in this country too
I care about my safety and every single one of my crew
I care about the kids on the play ground
I care about the old and the new
I care about the economy and the politics
I care about taxes and inflation
Tuition fees and education
See let me repeat, I LIVE HERE TOO

If my neighbour died, I would cry and be sad too
If my community was hurt, I'd be hurt too
Don't judge me because of the few
I know my culture, respect my religion, but I love this
country too
I go to school and contribute my knowledge
I work hard so I can pay for my daughter's college
Pay taxes and vote, because remember. I LIVE IN THIS
COUNTRY TOO

We don't judge all Germans because of Nazis and Hitler
So why judge Muslims because of bin Laden and Taliban
But not use the KKK to judge every white man.
I'm not Eurocentric, nor a terrorist
I'm a human being speaking the truth without being
centrist
I'm a Muslim, I'm a Canadian, I'm a global being
Regardless of what I've known and seen
I'll always be a human being
Against violence, killing and corrupt regimes
Against stereotypes and false accusation
Against injustice and discrimination
I stand for humanity when I say
That we Muslims may have a different way
But in every culture and religion there is white black
and grey

I'm an immigrant who's travelled different realms
Came to this country with many dreams
Instead I am
looked down at as a minority
Because I refuse conformity

I'm going to bring about my visibility
Outgrow the system and create a new community
Beat the media and stereotypes
And achieve superiority
I'll be calling it **human-o-archy**

Democracy, is it?

Although written many years ago, I still relate to this next poem. I was confused about what is right and what is wrong, divided on whether it's my religion or culture that is wrong or if it's ultimately a corrupt system. I hope it will inspire you to truly question what is really happening around you, and although questions may not yield answers right away, it's the questioning in itself that opens up a world of light, growth, wisdom and an overall understanding of the world around us, regardless of who we are and where we come from.

Democracy ... or so they say
I look at our countries and they lag behind
I look at my people and I see pain in their eyes
I look around and see clear air and blue skies
Mercedes, Lamborghinis, and Ferraris, of all colours
Versace, Gucci purses and jeans of all styles
People with coloured drinks in their hands
swallowing pill of all kinds
Then I get all confused,
go home with a list of questions in my mind
Is it us or is it them?
Blood rushes to my head, tears fill my eyes, anguish,
anger emotions of all kind.
Is it anger, hate, fear or pain coming around?
Am I blind or just seen too much?
Oh God, stop it, I'm losing it, what's going on?

They tell me not to question,
they tell me to mould to their kind
But I refuse to see what they want me to see
I refuse to live in a painting they call art
See ...
Gandhi was thought to be weak, since he didn't eat meat,
And practise all the "reformations"
the British brought along
But he left a changed world behind
Martin Luther king was a man of all time,
Because he also left a changed world behind
Except he made his colour visible even
to those that were blind

So it's not colour, it's not religion,
why they hating on my vision?
I got the mind of a Buddhist
I got the heart of a Muslim
I got a colour of no definition
I got one defined mission
To question a painting even when
not given permission
See I'm one of those that believes in my intuition
It's not my Islam my country or
my people that are wrong
It's the system that is corrupt

It's economic, political, sociological psychological institutions
They all be bringing dynamic, abstract, fearful, ambitious, apathetic confusions

Oh God, not again ... why how when where and why?
... but ... that ... just ... all ...
... it just doesn't ... just doesn't ...
... doesn't make sense.

Walking Away

Pain can easily take the form of anger. Like fuel to an engine, our pain and our happiness are both used to fuel our soul and to help us grow. In this next poem, although the words seem like those of someone cold and strong, you can sense a girl who is truly scared, someone who is speaking strong words so she can heal, someone who is trying hard to convince herself that she's walking away from being hurt. You can sense that this woman is fed up and has had enough. She is divided between being alone or staying with someone whom she knows is unworthy. Her words are full of anger and bitterness, yet she knows that her choice to walk away is the right one, because true love should not make you angry or bitter.

Complicated as it seems
Things have never been so clear
To all the men I was ever near
Here are a few words I would like you to hear

I was always nice and respectful
Patient and grateful, never neglectful
I made you smile when I even couldn't
I was honest when you even weren't
Accepted your lies, although I shouldn't
I gave you what other girls wouldn't
Sweetness, love, strength, and faith in Allah the above

I gave you a mother's love
A friend's acceptance
A wise man's tolerance
A brother's loyalty
I was a star in your night
And a warm breeze in your day
And now for all of the above
I have to pay

You're not worth it
I'm proud to say
So it's time for you to let me go and walk away

Better to be alone than unappreciated
Better to smile and be anticipated
Than be caught up in something that my heart has
degenerated

You're selfish and cold-hearted
But your charm had me blind-sighted
I painted a fake picture of who I wanted you to be
But the whole time my brain was only fooling me

Don't get me wrong or get mad
But you're just not the best I had
Nor the best I want to have
You were just there
And made me laugh
I figured I could use something new
And you stood out amongst the few
But like the shirt I bought last year
I was happy with it
Until the shirt I saw in the window this year

Women

From a very young age, I thought of women as
something great! I hated watching women look
weak: I wanted them all to always stand tall, know
their rights, and speak their thoughts. I was born in
a place where women were assigned specific roles
and no matter how intelligent or capable they were,
they were never given what they deserved. Coming
to Canada, I thought maybe women would be given
more. Yet I came to realize that what is thought of as
freedom—the ability to wear and say what we want—
was just the tip of the iceberg and that the issues
are much deeper than what we are allowed to wear
or say. Inequality of women is something that still
persists, and I say hats off to the women fighting for
our equality every day. I am a born feminist and every
day I challenge what I was taught about how women
should be, since I believe that there are no limits to
what a woman can be.

Women ARE the teachers of tomorrow's civilization.
They are the ones who raise our children, they are the
ones who share their men's decisions, they are lawyers,
doctors and CEOs. They nurture and take care of others.
Women are mothers, daughters, and sisters. They take
care of you when you're sick, call you out when you're
wrong and not speak to you when you mess up.

Women have made great men and nurtured great civilizations. Women have done what no man has done: give birth. They have loved, earned their education, and built corporations. A woman is more than a sex symbol; a woman is a temple, she is a sensual creation, her body is a work of art, her spirit is purity. A woman is not a "bitch"; a woman is a sweet, gentle and warm-hearted being whose hug can cure what ails you.

A woman is a mother who will raise poets, doctors, teachers, and talented people. She is the most important being in this universe and without her, there is no beauty. So how is it that our society has come this far only to forget who women are? Why is it that women today can't look in the mirror and realize that they were once queens, and mothers of great emperors? Women, you are tomorrow, you are love, you are life.

My Constitution

Overwhelmed by a slew of information and beliefs and opinions as a child, I decided to write my very own constitution which I have lived and continue to live my life by!

Don't take my sweetness for weakness ... don't mistake my smile for ignorance
Don't tell me how to behave, show me how you do
Don't forget who you are or from where you came
Don't lose your soul because you'll have only yourself to blame
Don't fall under pressure, don't sell yourself cheap
Don't let your heart die or forget what you believe
For it is the believing that lifts you up when no one else does

Don't let others walk on you because of your faith
Don't let others kill your soul and break your heart
Because a soul only dies once and a heart will continue
to beat
Each giving you more time to heal

Don't seek money, seek knowledge
Don't seek power, seek respect
Don't be envious, be glad
Don't be ashamed, be proud
You have your health
You have those whom you love
And those who love you
You have food
You have clothes
You have money
And much more

Be thankful
And let others be
Focus on yourself and let your soul rest free
Remember who you are
And I promise
YOU'LL SMILE JUST LIKE ME

Forbidden Truth

This next poem is about the thoughts rushing through my mind after doing something that was forbidden. Divided between feelings of transgression and pleasure, this is the voice that speaks to me from within.

Uttering words with no sound
No one can hear but the person inside
Emotionless times, passionate feelings
Forbidden Truth

Reality becomes a dream
A dream becomes a moment
A moment lasts for seconds each with more pleasure
Each contaminated
Because that minute has in it withheld
The reality of the
Forbidden Truth

Beware

The following poem examines one of the divisions
that motivates so many of our actions, the one
between love and fear, through the words below I
describe myself in terms of good versus bad. Looking
at this writing now, I can sense that I was longing
to love and be loved, but I fear myself. I am warning
someone that I may be bad for him, almost like this
is my way of pushing him away before he can even
begin to love me. (you can tell I was my own judge,
and a very harsh judge)

I may kiss like a wondrous mistress
Yet I may poison you like a jungle snake

I may smile with innocence
Yet I maybe the definition of corruption

I may be the only truth you heard
Yet I may be the only lie you have known

I may be the sun that brightens your day
Yet I may be your darkness for life

I may touch you like a mother
Yet I may scar every inch of your soul

Reflection

Another division is very obvious in this next poem. I am describing a lover as someone who is everything good and everything bad ... or am I describing myself?

You are the medicine that my heart seeks
You are the poison before every night's sleep
You are the reflection of my pain
Yet you are the only joy for my eyes to see

You are my screams of torture and hurt
Yet you are the smile of happiness and peace

You are the corruption of my brain
Yet you are the angel in me

You are my tears, my cry of pain
Yet you are my excitement, bliss and pleasure
You are me trapped in you
Yet you are you trapped in me
Your brain is mine and mine is yours
Yet neither yours nor mine

Change

There isn't much I can say about the next poem, except that it can be summed up as a common term we use in marketing—it's a call to action!

A world filled with discrimination
War all over the nation

Innocent children dying of starvation
Bombs ruining God's creation

Stop, let's act
And create a rotation
Search for actions
And generate imitations
Of what was once known as a human-God relation
Jot it down and put it into a notation
Maybe one day
You yourself and I will get a standing ovation.

Intuition

The next short poem I simply call intuition—
remember, you are what you create!

Admiration of beauty leads to things beyond description
Then those descriptions become scripts into an
imagination
Soon to be reality of beyond controllable feelings
Unforgettable experience

Remember

This is simply dedicated to any woman who has suffered any abuse, especially physical abuse. To any mother who tried to protect her children but could not protect herself, I want you to read this and remember that you are more than good enough. That you are worthy, and beyond all that you are perfect just the way you are. I had been through a very abusive relationship and was lucky to get out before I was killed. I had nights crying and feeling so weak, so I wrote this to myself to help me get strength to get to another day.

REMEMBER that while your tears fall, he still feels
pleasure

REMEMBER when you shake and your
breath stops, that he holds another

REMEMBER that his words may be
sweet but his fists weren't

REMEMBER what he claims but what
he delivered

REMEMBER when your about to give
up that your a mother

A Letter to my Daughter

Dear beautiful,

A few things I would like to leave you with

Love yourself, love your soul, because when you do, you will have passion and drive for life.
When life senses the energy of love radiating from within you,
then life will love you back, it will blow the essence of it's eternal love into you,
so that even when your no longer alive, you live.

Once I stopped surviving, I started living, I hope that I
can give you a life that
you do not have to think and aim to just survive,
but rather your survival is a given, and so life is your
purpose, to live
it with a cause;
so make sure you choose a cause that gives you endless
hope.
Make it close to your heart,
but make sure you are passionate about it, and let it
keep you authentic so you
can stay true to yourself.

Yourself and who you are, are two different things.
Yourself is your material self, your body, and your mind.
Who you are is much bigger than that. Who you are
within is a spark of energy that came from an
eternal, infinite pool of energy (God), and although this
spark may seem so
little because of our physical bodies, but the power it
withholds is beyond our imagination.
Use your imagination wise, imagine things that are
unimaginable,
because I am here to tell you that they are attainable my
love.

Seek life so it can also seek you, find life so it finds you,
don't wait for life to happen to you,
make yourself happen to life.

Habits, we are creatures of habit, please make sure you developed good habits,
and feed into good practices. Ensure you develop habits to feed the three things that complete your perfection
in the physical world. Your mind, you body and your soul.

Feed your mind with knowledge, always learn , always read, always ask
Feed your body with health, feed it nourishing food , drink lots of water, and moisturize.
Move your muscles, work out parts you don't use, keep moving.
Feed your soul, with love, with acts of kindness, with prayers, with meditation,
with laughter, with passion, with human touch and connections.

I love you more than words will ever express

THE BEGINNING...

I don't want to use the term "the end," nor "conclusion." I find both to be limiting: there is no ending to our learning and there are no conclusions that are final. Instead, I wanted to conclude this writing by referring to it as the "beginning."

Looking back on these writings has made me truly face myself, and through them I have learned about different aspects of my personality, my struggles, my pains, and my joy. They helped me survive hard experiences, and through words I was able to let my emotion out on paper so I am able to function in life regardless of what I was undergoing.

After going through all of the writing and putting the pieces of where they originated together, I was able to truly heal and come to peace with much of my pain. For me, this is just the beginning: our past doesn't determine our future, but when we use it wisely, it can definitely influence it in more positive ways than negative ones.

Many of us seek progress and we may think this comes only through hard work, education, etc. However, progress as a whole human comes from emotional wellbeing. Internal health creates power beyond anything that is external. When achieved, all that is external becomes easier. The universe has somehow guided me to open old chapters of my life and look back at my emotional ride and come to terms with my pain and my past. I pray that through sharing it with you, some of you may relate to the pain, loneliness, the joy, the struggle, and could also face them and come to peace with them so you can harvest a new form of emotional power that will lead you to your higher self. We sometimes spend years escaping pain, but it is only when we face our fear that we can conquer it. So face your pain and conquer it to open your heart to limitless feelings of joy.

Here's to a new beginning and limitless joy,

J.